TRANSLATORS, TRAITORS

ERIC ENGLE

Copyright © 2021

amazon.com/author/quizmaster

Introduction

How did China go from being a country on the brink of starvation to the world's largest economy? How did the USA go from being the world's largest economy to a deindustrialized, unemployed, overweight, diabetic, drug addicted nation losing war after endless war where mass murder shooting sprees are normal with the largest prison population on earth in absolute and per capita terms? Are these coincidences or are they causally connected, and if so: how?

"Translators Traitors" tells one small part of the story of the destruction of the USA and the rise of China. It is one in a series of books which describes the various aspects of the destruction of the greatest democracy in human history and its replacement by the largest and most powerful dictatorship in human history. Other books in this series are presented at the end of this livret.

TABLE OF CONTENTS

CHAPTER 1.
MISTRANSLATIONS

子曰、非礼 勿视、非礼勿听、非礼勿言、非礼勿动。

Zǐ yuē, fēilǐ wù shì, fēilǐ wù tīng, fēilǐ wù yán, fēilǐ wù dòng.

"The words of Confucius: Do not look at that which is improper, do not listen to that which is improper, do not say that which is improper, and do not do that which is improper." Analects

Is it too late? Outdated? Already irrelevant? Or does Deng Xiaoping stand out to this day as crucial to comprehending contemporary China?

Deng Xiaoping is both the person responsible for the massacre of Chinese pro-democracy protestors at Tiananmen Square and also the economic reformer who championed Chinas "reform and opening up" putting China on a state capitalist path. Dr. Jekill and Mr. Hide?

Since then of course, Xi Jinping has abolished the politburo, centralized power, and is bringing greater state control and surveillance over industry and business. How much of it is personal political ambition? Probably much of it. How much of it is conscious political strategy? Much there too, perhaps even most of it. Xi could never centralize so much political power in his own hands with no coherent rational national strategy. Though, at least Xi Jinping did not massacre Hong Kong's protestors. In that sense, so far, he is better htan Deng.

So, is Lenin right? Is the march of history really "Two steps forward, one step back?"

Liberal democracies believed that fostering economic growth in China would lead to the attainment of peace and prosperity which in turn would result in greater human rights recognition and protection as well as democratization. All those Western hopes proved to have been an illusion. China is moving toward greater authoritarianism with increased international security conflicts, greater state intervention in the economy, and little or no hope of improved human rights, let alone democratization despite strikingeconomic improvement. Even attainment of the rule of law in China can be seriously questioned now as the cult of personality returns. To centralize power in his own hands, Xi Jinping is clearly willing to kill the goose that lays the golden eggs, whether in Hong Kong or at Jack Ma's Alibaba. In fact, China's international economic initiatives, the belt and road initiative and the Asian Infrastructure and Investment Bank specifically disavow concerns with human rights, democracy, or the rule of law. Foreign policies generally speaking for any country reflect domestic policies. Finally, China builds artificial islands, makes ridiculous territorial claims, and is arms racing. So much for peace and prosperity, human rights and democracy, through trade development and interdependence. The failure of liberal internationalism could not be more evident.

How was the West so badly deluded? Much of its folly was the product of convenient self deception. It was all too easy to ignore the fact that cheap Chinese products were and are so cheap because they are produced by slave labor with little or no work-place safety. Feasting on slave labor placated American workers as their jobs were "outsourced", lost, sent to cheaper factories in China. They had more tools and toys which surely muted working class discontent with reduced pay and perks as unions were smashed and factory jobs shipped overseas. The feast on slave labor feast also funded that wonderful Wall Street stock market bull, so elites were even more pleased than the unemployed. The vast growing income gap between elites and workers in the USA was papered over with cheap Chinese swag. Real wealth was rising even among the poor although workers wages and relative wealth of workers in the USA as compared to the rich in America was declining. But this festival of consumption was founded on Chinese slave labor. Yet, though America was fat dumb and happy the Chinese government was shrewd. Thin profit margins but mass quantities of sales were smartly reinvested into Chinese industries and, more ominously, the Chinese military.

Consequently, China now has the world's largest economy, the world's largest navy, and is challenging the US for global hegemony. The illusions have been largely -- not entirely! -- dispelled: there is still plenty of greedy wishful thinking. Only the willfully blind have failed to notice the mask of Chinese subservience and conformity with free trade and open borders dropped. Mercantilist state capitalism, not liberal free trade, is the economic ideology directing the Chinese economy, and it has been wildly successful, at least until 2020 due to the wishful thinking Western unicorn liberalism.

Part of the grand illusion was the product of bad translations. Since I actually read Chinese I thought to present what you were told the Chinese government was saying as opposed to what the Chinese were actually saying -- and doing -- while your job was being sent to Shanghai.

The process of economic reform in China is referred to in English as "Reform and opening up". Here already we encounter the first bad translation. "Reform and opening up" is a translation of "gaige kaifang" 改革開放: while kaifang does mean "opening up" 改革 gaige breaks down to "change revolution". Whether you like or hate revolutions or are indifferent (they are wild affairs) 改革 definitely connotes the idea of a radical change. In other words, it can be interpreted as: the revolution moves forward. By the way, this particular revolution is intended to install proletarian communist dictatorships and replace the US as global hegemon, fyi.

It may be putting to much faith or trust in epigrams take the now dated Quotations of Chairman Deng Xiaoping seriously. It is all too easy to read too much into any epigram. Epigrams are popular precisely because they allow the reader to insert their own ideas and then have a sense of (possibly false) triumph and comprehension. Epigrams are not always or only "glittering generalities" but to the extent they are not mere propaganda they only set out general guidelines, directives for the implementation and execution of state policies and laws. Yet, these epigrams are nonetheless preciuous: They are the few governing principles which escape from the black box of democratic centralism, the "tea leaves" we try to read. It's not helped by hopeful mistranslation.

But wait: it gets worse. Intrepreting "revolutionary reform and opening" as "reform and opening up" is one of the nicer bad translations.

CHAPTER 2.
DENG'S APHORISMS

Deng's 24 character aphorisms are: 冷静观察, 站稳脚跟, 沉着应付, 韬光养晦, 善于守拙, 绝不当头

Here's what the USA Pentagon thinks Deng said, supposedly based on CCP documents:

"Observe calmly; secure our position; cope with affairs calmly; hide our capacities and bide our time; be good at maintaining a low profile; and never claim leadership." (冷静观察, 站稳脚跟, 沉着应付, 韬光养晦, 善于守拙, 绝不当头) --Deng Xiaoping (early 1990s)

Department of Defense, Annual Report to Congress: Military Power of the People's Republic of China 2008

www.defenselink.mil/pubs/pdfs/China_Military_Report_08.pdf (30 MB)

If only.

Deng came up with six principles all right. But the Pentagon's translations are ... wrong.

1) leng jing guan cha 冷静观察 is better translated as: observe and examine [critically] [with a] cool [head] here's the tones for those who care: Lěngjìng guānchá = stay out of trouble, don't get trolled or psyched out. This reminds us of the East Asian saying "the hammer which sticks out gets nailed down". Deng's strategies are conservative and seek the long term survival of his own faction and the CCP. This does not however mean they are passive or purely defensive, let alone that they will magically transform a communist dictatorship into a capitalist liberal democracy, wishful thinking of Wall Street and some beltway bandits to the contrary.

2) 站稳脚跟 Zhàn wěn jiǎogēn is better translated as "stand firmly [on your] foothold" i.e. don't back down when challenged, don't lose gained ground. Deng here is arguing that the advance of China, the CCP, and the international communist movement (ICM) should operate like a ratchet, going one way, only. Whatever gains have been made are not to be sacrificed. "Secure

our position" might be true as far as it goes, but does not go far enough and is in any case inaccurate.

3) 沉着应付 Chénzhuó yìngfù lit. "deep strategy should pay" i.e. pay careful regard to strategic depth. This is both an admonition about the submarine navy and also a strategic dictum. It means: Deng, the CCP and China are playing the long game. Whoever translated that as "deal with challenges in peace and quiet" is worse than wrong, they are a saboteur. There's no way chen shuo ying fu translates into "deal with challenges in peace and quiet". "Deep Trick Should Pay" is what it literally says. You could translate it as "cope calmly" but the way to cope is: Deep strategic trickery. 着 is polyphonic. The tone change makes it a different word. One meaning is trickery, another drama, another groping about half blind for a solution. More context is needed for this one, like all the other aphorisms. However it does not merely mean "cope with affairs calmly".

Chinese words rarely translate one-for-one with English words. They generally cover a range of meanings, with several possible corresponding English terms. Generally speaking, Chinese words arose as literal objects and activities in the real world. These literals then accrued implied and metaphoric meanings. This process of accretion of meaning dependant on context is why our translation tables are rarely or even nearly never one-for-one, term-for-term. This is part of why Chinese is a challenge and adventure. Another part is the characters: Every character is a picture, a puzzle, a story, and an adventure adding depth and meaning to the otherwise epigrammatic. I love it, you should learn it, and good luck!

4) 韬光养晦 Tāo guāng yǎng huì is purportedly officially translated as: "Bide our time and build up our capabilities." That's not what it really says. It literally says: "Sheath Light Raise Blind" In other words: "Cover [your] light, foster blindness. The word cover here can also be translated as "sheath" i.e. do not use one's own violence, so sometimes the bad translations also hide things which benefit the CCP. After all, a blind adversary need not be killed.

5) 善于守拙 "virtue at honest poverty". That's what it says all right. Shànyú shǒu zhuō This aphorism is correctly admonishing the CCP to recognize and respect the spartan virtues which brought it to power. The party is to be benevolent toward the poor, its ultimate constituent and legitimator. Against true virtue I am powerless.

6) 绝不当头 literally "cut short not as head" i.e. don't stick your neck out, don't be obvious, conform and obey. Again, whoever is "translating" this is either doing so in massive context with a lot more text than just these cheng yu OR they are lying. It's probably both. Is this an admonition for the party members with respect to the party leadership? Is it an admonition to the Chinese Ministry of Foreign affairs in its dealings with the US and NATO? Is it both? And more? Aphorisms conceal as much they reveal and enable us to input our own content -- which may or may not then be extended, distended, or outright refuted.

You must read much into these aphorisms for them to make any sense. Yet, you cannot read too much into them. In other words: literary and political contexts are necessary in order to understand the significance of these aphorisms.

However, the bad translations of these aphorisms, some of which are clearly directed against US interests and most or even all of which are aimed at the survival of the CCP in the wake of the collapse of the CPUSSR partly explains why the US is now face to face with 30+ years of failed China policy.

This dark discussion of the contention for state power must seem like I've opened Pandora's box for you. Each of the beautiful hopeful aphorisms which would be shown to promise you peace through prosperity and interdepence by free trade has turned out to be nothing more or less than a strategic or tactical guide for the party state to survive and contend against liberal democracies, a poisoned chalice.

Yet, like Pandora's box, there is also hope: the legitimator and truest constituent of the impossible communist ideal is the world's poor. If the party state is to be redeemed it will be through its salvation of the world's poor. As they say,

It is not enough to fix the old broken world.

We must also build up a happy new world.

But as well as hope, I must also leave you this warning:

Hope dies last.

Chapter 3. The Diplomatic and Strategic Significance of the Translation of the Chinese Vocabulary "Hide One's Capacity and Bide Your Time"

I am not the only person to have noticed how badly translated Deng's aphorisms are. Xiong Guangkai in Public Diplomacy Quarterly in May 31, 2010 wrote the following.

Key Point: "Keeping a low profile" has become an important part of China's foreign strategic policy, and it is also one of the keywords for understanding and grasping China's foreign policy. A correct understanding and accurate translation of "hide your capacities and bide your time" will help to better introduce China's peaceful foreign policy to the outside world, promote the international community's understanding of China's peaceful development path and traditional strategic culture, and maintain and further shape China's good international image. [In other words: The CCP, a single party dictatorship, is going nowhere.]

In the late 1980s and early 1990s, Comrade Deng Xiaoping put forward the diplomatic strategy of "hiding our capacities and biding our time" based on a profound understanding of China's national conditions and a comprehensive grasp of the world situation. To this day, "hiding one's capacity and biding one's time" has become an important part of China's foreign strategic policy, and it is also one of the key words to understand and grasp China's foreign policy. At present, the relationship between China and the world has undergone historic changes, and the overall interaction between the domestic and international situations has become increasingly close. The correct understanding and accurate translation of the term "hide one's capacity and bide time" will undoubtedly help to better introduce China's peaceful foreign policy to the outside world, promote the international community's understanding of China's peaceful development path and traditional strategic culture, and maintain and further shape China Good international image. This is exactly a problem that we need to pay attention to and solve in public diplomacy.

Misinterpretation of "Hiding One's Capacity"

Regrettably, for many years, many people in the West have suffered from inaccurate translation and even misinterpretation when interpreting the term "hide one's capacity and bide one's time". These wrong translations and interpretations are often used by forces with ulterior motives to attack and discredit

China and promote the "China threat theory." For example, in the "Report on China's Military Power" published by the US Department of Defense for the first time in 2002, it specifically quoted and emphasized Comrade Deng Xiaoping's past "Calm Observation, Calmness to Deal with, Steady Positions, Keep a Low Profile, Never Take the Lead, and Make a Difference. "Hide our capabilities and bide our time" in English as "hide our capabilities and bide our time", which means "cover one's abilities and wait for the opportunity to make a comeback." Since then, the U.S. government has adopted the same English expression in the "Report on China's Military Power" for six years, including 2003, 2004, 2005, 2006, 2007, and 2009. In addition, there are some English books or articles abroad that translate "Hide one's ability and pretend to be weak", meaning "conceal one's ability and pretend to be weak"; "conceal one's true intention", meaning "hide true intentions"; "hide one's ambitions and disguise its claws", which means "hide one's ambitions and disguise its claws". The above and so on, and so on, the subtext is nothing more than: "Keeping a low profile" is an expedient measure adopted by China in a specific internal and external situation. It is "concealing one's true intentions" and "waiting for the time to come." to take another shot.

Undoubtedly, these interpretations have completely distorted the connotation and essence of China's strategic policy of peaceful diplomacy, and have caused undue negative effects on our normal diplomatic relations. I have explained and explained this issue many times when I visited abroad and participated in some academic exchange activities at home and abroad. In 2006, during my visit to the United States by a delegation from the Chinese Institute of Foreign Affairs, I had a meeting with former U.S. Secretary of State Schultz, Kissinger, and former ambassador to China Rui Xiaojian, among others, and specifically pointed out that the U.S. government stated in the "Report on China's Military Strength" The translation is wrong, and the US should pay attention to this issue to avoid causing strategic misjudgments by both sides and affecting the overall situation of the stable development of Sino-US relations.

The Causes of Translation Errors in "Keeping a low profile"

It should be said that the reason why "hide your capacity and bide your time" has been misinterpreted and condemned by the West deeply reflects the inherent political and strategic prejudice of some people in Western countries towards China, as well as the cold war mentality of a few anti-China forces. There are also omissions in translation and interpretation related to deviations [i.e. errors within the CCP and its mass organizations with understanding and/or implementing its political line]. For example, the "New Century Chinese-English Dictionary" published by Foreign Language Teaching and Research Press in 2006 translated [the Chinese term into] "hide one's capabilities and bide one's time". The Chinese-English bilingual "Chinese Wisdom in Life" published by Foreign Languages Publishing House in 2007 explained "keeping a low profile" as "a strategy to behave". "When the time is not yet ripe, it is best to hide your talents and wait for the right opportunity". The corresponding English expression is "to conceal one's fame and ability"; "temporary retirement to bide one's time before going on the offensive". [I.e. the difference between a defensive or offensive protracted strategy]

The reason for this misunderstanding can be roughly attributed to the following two reasons. One is the misunderstanding of the idiom "hide our power and bide our time". In essence, "keeping a low profile" means acting low-key and modest. This is a kind of life virtue and philosophical thought that our Chinese nation has always advocated, and it cannot be equated to "conspiracy" and "drilling camp" and other life tricks. [I.e. a defensive strategy for self-regulation as opposed to an offenive policy of waiting in ambush.] There are also people who mistakenly equated "hiding one's capacity and biding time" with "deserving courage". As we all know, "Let's take courage" tells the story of the King Goujian of Yue and his revenge and hatred during the Spring and Autumn Period. Therefore, "hiding one's capacity and biding one's time" is associated with the so-called "waiting for the opportunity" and "revanche". This incorrect understanding and interpretation should not be used as the basis for the translation of important words. The second is the misunderstanding of the diplomatic strategic thinking of "hiding our capacities and biding our time". "Keeping a low profile" is an important foreign strategic policy of our country, and it is by no means a temporary strategy or expedient. Comrade Deng Xiaoping's "hide our capacities and bide our time" has rich and profound connotations. It not only has profound historical background, but also conforms to the national conditions and world conditions. He emphasizes that we should keep a low profile, be modest and prudent, not seek hegemony or engage in confrontation, concentrate on economic development, and single-mindedly seek Peaceful development [i.e. consistent with China's mission to end global poverty]. China pursues the foreign strategic policy of "hiding one's capacity and biding time". The starting point is not to "stand by and then strike" or "revanchism", but rather to emphasize the need to seize the current period of important strategic opportunities for national development, realize the great rejuvenation of the Chinese nation, and promote the peaceful development of the world. This is an indisputable fact that has been repeatedly proved by China's diplomatic practice over the years.

Correctly translating the diplomatic strategic significance of "hide our capacities and bide our time":

Fortunately, in September 2009, the sixth edition of "Ci Hai" published by Shanghai Lexicographic Publishing House, edited by Comrade Chen Zhili, added the phrase "hide one's capacity and bide time" for the first time, which was interpreted as "hiding talents and not revealing them". Related interpretations also include: "sheath" refers to "quiver" and means "to hide"; "Tao Guang" refers to "condensing brilliance", metaphorically "hiding reputation and talent"; "Tao Hui" refers to "converging edge." , Hiding in order to walk". It can be seen that the core meaning of "hiding one's capacity and biding one's time" is to not show one's strengths, but there is no meaning of "covering up attempts" or "waiting for a comeback." The accurate interpretation in the sixth edition of "Ci Hai" provides an authoritative basis for us to better understand China's foreign strategic policy and to better carry out foreign exchanges and public diplomacy. According to the interpretation of "Ci Hai", the accurate translation of "hide one's capacity and bide time" will greatly reduce the misunderstanding and estrangement in cross-cultural communication.

I also noticed that [Fareed] Zakaria, the editor-in-chief of the international edition of Newsweek, wrote a book entitled "The Post-American World" in 2008. He also cited "hiding one's light" when discussing China's foreign strategic policy, and the English translation he used was "hiding one's light". This translation is derived from a passage in the "Bible": "Neither do men light a candle, and put it under a bushel, but on a candlestick; and it giveth light unto all that are in the house." (Note: giveth is Old English, with the same semantics as give). In Chinese this can be translated as "When a person lights a lamp, not under the bucket, but on the lampstand, it illuminates the family." Later generations extended the above allusion to the proverb "hide one's light under a bushel" meaning to diffuse sharp edges. However, the translation of "hiding one's light" is still inaccurate. Nevertheless, this practice of borrowing well-known allusions in Western culture for translating Chinese idioms according to Western thinking habits has brought us useful enlightenment. In the past, we also used "keep a low profile" ... but there is still a certain distance from fully accurate expression of its meaning, and foreigners still have difficulty understanding the original term's profound meaning.

How to translate terms such as "hide our powers and bide our time" which involve China's diplomatic strategy and policy is of great importance. Based on accurately grasping the authoritative interpretation of these words, we should strive to use careful rather than careless, lively rather than stiff, and use fine rather than blunt language to accurately express its due meaning. This is of great importance to better promote public diplomacy and shape China's good international image.

General Xiong Guangkai, former Deputy Chief of Staff of the Chinese People's Liberation Army.

Chapter 4. General Xiong's Essay in Response to the Pentagon's Mistranslation of Deng's Aphorisms

熊光楷：中文词汇"韬光养晦"翻译的外交战略意义2010年05月31日 17:33公共外交季刊【大 中 小】【打印】共有评论1条

核心提示："韬光养晦"已成为中国对外战略方针的重要组成部分，也是理解和把握中国外交政策的关键词之一。正确理解和准确翻译"韬光养晦"，将有助于更好地向外界介绍中国的和平外交政策，促进国际社会对中国和平发展道路和传统战略文化的了解，维护并进一步塑造中国良好的国际形象。

20世纪80年代末90年代初，邓小平同志基于对中国国情的深刻认识和世界局势的全面把握，提出了"韬光养晦"的外交战略思想。时至今日，"韬光养晦"已成为中国对外战略方针的重要组成部分，也是理解和把握中国外交政策的关键词之一。当前，中国与世界的关系发生了历史性变化，国内国际两个大局互动日益紧密。对"韬光养晦"一词的正确理解和准确翻译，无疑将有助于更好地向外界介绍中国的和平外交政策，促进国际社会对中国和平发展道路和传统战略文化的了解，维护并进一步塑造中国良好的国际形象。这也正是我们在公共外交中需要重视和解决的一个问题。

对"韬光养晦"的曲解

令人遗憾的是，多年来不少西方人士在解读"韬光养晦"一词时，或多或少存在着翻译不准确，甚至曲解的现象。这些错误的译法和解读又往往被一些别有用心的势力所利用，以此来攻击抹黑中国、鼓吹"中国威胁论"。例如，美国国防部在2002年首次公布的《中国军力报告》中，就专门引用并特别强调了邓小平同志过去提出的"冷静观察、沉着应付、稳住阵脚、韬光养晦、决不当头、有所作为"等战略方针，其中"韬光养晦"所用英文为"hide our capabilities and bide our time"，意即"掩盖自己的能力，等待时机东山再起"。此后，美国政府在2003年、2004年、2005年、2006年、2007年和2009年等六个年度的《中国军力报告》中都采用了同样的英文表述。另外，国外还有一些英文书籍或文章将"韬光养晦"译为"hide one's ability and pretend to be weak"，意即"隐藏能力、假装弱小"；"conceal one's true intention"，意即"隐藏真实目的"；"hide one's ambitions and disguise its claws"，意即"隐藏野心、收起爪子"。以上等等，不一而足，其中的潜台词无外乎："韬光养晦"是中国在特定的内外形势下所采取的一种权宜之计，是在"隐蔽自己的真实意图"，"等待时机成熟再出手"。

无庸置疑，上述这些解读完全歪曲了中国和平外交战略方针的内涵和实质，给我们的正常对外交往造成了不应有的负面影响。我在出国访问和参加国内外一些学术交流活动时，多次就这一问题做过解释和说明。2006年，我在中国外交学会代表团赴美访问期间，与美前国务卿舒尔茨、基辛格和前驻华大使芮效俭等会谈时专门提出，美国政府在《中国军力报告》中对"韬光养晦"的翻译是错误的，美方应当重视这一问题，避免因此引发双方的战略误判，影响中美关系稳定发展的大局。

"韬光养晦"翻译偏差的原因

应该说，"韬光养晦"之所以被西方曲解责难，一方面深刻反映了西方国家一些人士对华固有的政治战略偏见，以及少数反华势力顽固坚持的冷战思维，另一方面也与我们国内对"韬光养晦"的翻译和解释存在疏漏与偏差有关。例如，外语教学与研究出版社2006年出版的《新世纪汉英大辞典》，就将"韬光养晦"翻译为"hide one's capabilities and bide one's time"，这与美国《中国军力报告》中的译法几乎一样。外文出版社2007年出版的中英对照《生活中的中国智慧》

一书，将"韬光养晦"解释为"一种为人的策略"，"在时机尚未成熟时，最好先隐藏自己的才能，等待合适的机会"。其对应的英文表述是"to conceal one's fame andability"；"temporary retirement to bide one's time before goingon the offensive"。

之所以会出现这样的误解，大致可以归结为以下两个原因。一是对"韬光养晦"这一成语的理解有误。从本质上说，"韬光养晦"是指行事低调、谦让。这是我们中华民族历来倡导的一种人生美德和哲学思想，不可等同于"阴谋""钻营"等处世伎俩。也有人错误地将"韬光养晦"与"卧薪尝胆"相提并论。众所周知，"卧薪尝胆"讲的是春秋时期越王勾践复仇雪恨的故事，因此"韬光养晦"就被联想演绎出了所谓"等待时机""东山再起"之意。这种不正确的理解和演绎，不应作为重要词语翻译的依据。二是对"韬光养晦"外交战略思想的理解有误。"韬光养晦"是我国重要的对外战略方针，决非一时的策略和权宜之计。邓小平同志提出的"韬光养晦"内涵丰富而深刻，既有深厚的历史底蕴，也符合国情和世情，强调我们应保持低调，谦虚谨慎，不称霸，不搞对抗，集中精力抓好经济建设，一心一意谋求和平发展。中国奉行"韬光养晦"的对外战略方针，出发点不是所谓"待机而动""东山再起"，而恰恰是强调要抓住当前国家发展的重要战略机遇期，实现中华民族的伟大复兴，推动世界和平发展。这已是被多年来中国的外交实践所反复证明的不争事实。

正确翻译"韬光养晦"的外交战略意义

可喜的是，2009年9月，上海辞书出版社出版的由陈至立同志担任主编的第6版《辞海》中，首次增加了"韬光养晦"的辞条，其解释为"隐藏才能，不使外露"。与此相关的释义还包括："韬"指"弓袋"，并有"掩藏"之意；"韬光"指"敛藏光彩"，比喻"掩藏声名才华"；"韬晦"指"收敛锋芒，隐藏才能行迹"。可见"韬光养晦"的核心含意就是不要锋芒毕露，完全没有"掩盖企图""等待东山再起"之意。第6版《辞海》的准确解释，为我们更好地理解中国对外战略方针，更好地开展对外交往和公共外交工作提供了权威依据。根据《辞海》的释义，再对"韬光养晦"进行准确翻译，将大大减少跨文化交流中出现的误解与隔阂。

我还注意到，美国《新闻周刊》国际版主编扎卡里亚2008年写了一本题为《后美国的世界》的书。他在论述中国对外战略方针时也引用了"韬光养晦"，而他使用的英文译法是"hiding its light"。这一译法源自《圣经》中的一段话："Neither do men light a candle, and put it undera bushel, but on a candlestick；and it giveth light unto all thatare in the house."（注：giveth为古体英语，与give语义相同）中文可译为"人点灯，不放在斗底下，是放在灯台上，就照亮一家的人。"后人将上述典故引申为谚语"hide one's light under a bushel"，意指不露锋芒。不过，用"hiding its light"来翻译"韬光养晦"仍有一些不确切。尽管如此，这种借用西方文化中众所周知的典故或是按西方思维习惯翻译中国成语的做法，给我们带来了有益启示。过去，我们也曾用"keep a lowprofile"（意为"保持低姿态、保持低调"）翻译"韬光养晦"，但这离完全准确表达其内涵也仍有一定距离，国外人士还难于理解到原词中深邃的含义。

可以说，如何翻译"韬光养晦"这样涉及中国外交战略方针的词语，关系重大。应在准确把握这些词语权威解释的基础上，力争运用精致的而不是粗疏的、活泼的而不是死板的、有亲和力的而不是生硬的外国语言，将其应有之义准确表达出来。这对于我们更好地推进公共外交、塑造中国的良好国际形象具有重要的意义。

熊光楷：本刊编委，中国国际战略研究基金会名誉会长，曾任中国人民解放军副总参谋长，上将军衔。

About the Author

Eric Engle studied law in the US, France, and Germany. He has taught law in France, Germany, Estonia, Russia, Ukraine, and Bosnia. A Fulbright law specialist and polyglot Dr. Engle really likes words.

Remember to learn more at
amazon.com/author/quizmaster

OTHER BOOKS BY ERIC ENGLE

A New Cold War Global Strategy (China, International Law, & Political Economy) (Nov 7, 2020)
A desperate dictatorship wracked by resource dependance. A distant democracy bent on isolationism and withdrawl from the violent turbulent world. New tactics, technologies, and weapons of war. Grand ambitions for cooperative regional development. Japan, 1941? China 2021?

Yes.

A New Cold War Global Strategy looks at the great power conflict between the US, Russia, and China. Examines parallels and divergences between current conflicts and past ones to determine the correct strategy for the US to manage its relations with China and Russia. Insights from history, economics, law, and philosophy combine to provide a good strategic roadmap for the United States.

200+ pages packed with insights and ideas from around the world throughout time. Free preview have a look inside and see for yourself!

- <u>Kindle</u>
  $0.00
  or $9.99 to buy
- <u>Paperback</u>
  $27.90

<u>Globalization with Chinese Characteristics: Liberalism, Nationalism, Realism, Marxism (China, International Law, & Political Economy)</u> (Jan 21, 2019)
by <u>Eric Engle</u>
A new cold war - with China? Globalization with Chinese characteristics studies China's global engagement to decipher china's grand strategy. China and the West are economic partners but security competitors. The Chinese economy is the material base of Chinese strategy: geoeconomics. Globalization with Chinese characterics explains China's future using geostrategy. Presents complex ideas simply and powerfully. Enables quick comprehension of US-Chinese relations and traces the contours of coming conflicts.
Click "look inside" for the *free* preview!

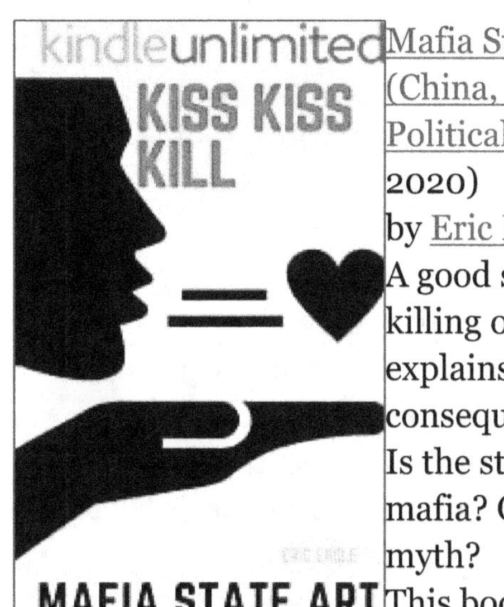

Mafia State Art Kiss Kiss Kill (China, International Law, & Political Economy) (Oct 23, 2020)

by Eric Engle (Author)

A good story starts with a killing or a kiss. It then explains its causes and consequences.
Is the state nothing but a mafia? Or is the mafia just a myth? This book will help you answer the questions so you can enjoy – or avoid! – state power.

What do Aristotle, Confucius, and Mao Zedong have to say about the state, art, and crime? Plenty!
Mafia, State, Art looks at the relationships between state power and crime with insights from Aristotle, Confucius, and Mao Zedong. And when it comes to bar trivia a good quotation from Chairman Mao always comes in hand for winning that bar bet!

Insightful and unusual, Mafia State Art gives an interesting perspective on the relationship between art and politics.

Kindle	
$6.66	See all buying options

[Gold, Geopolitics and Game Theory:: China & Investing Strategy (China, International Law, & Political Economy)](#)
(Mar 13, 2017)
by [Eric Engle (Author)](#)
Gold, Geopolitics and Game Theory: China and Investing Strategy shows readers how to identify and avoid mistakes in thinking about investing using game theory and mathematics. It shows links between gold, bitcoin, investing, trade, and foreign policy. Readily understood by novices, experts will find interesting insights herein. GGG was inspired by the late Orlin Grabbe, a libertarian economic analyst.

Kindle
$3.99

Read for Free

[Watergate 2.0: The Manchurian President? Trump's Radical Transformation of American Politics (China, International Law, & Political Economy)](#)
(Dec 2, 2017)
by [Eric Engle (Author)](#)
President Trump presents a radical rupture in American

political ideology and government policy, a shattering
of old values, old party lines, redrawing the political
map of America. Trump transforms both main
political parties. His rise reflects a deep
transformation in the American two-party system.
Whether Trump will be scapegoated by the system he
seeks to save or instead will ride to its rescue remains
to be seen. This book surveys the profound fault lines
Trump has riven and ridden in his ascent to American
power, explaining how and why both major parties
and the American polity will be forever changed
thanks to Trump -- no matter what his personal fate.

- <u>Paperback</u>
  $7.77

Why Trump Won, Why
Clinton Lost: How to Win an
Election (China, International
Law, & Political Economy)
(Mar 13, 2017)
by Eric Engle (Author)
How to Win an Election looks
at the qualities of leadership,
electoral tactics, and
campaign strategy, which
explain Why Clinton Lost and
How Trump Won.

See product details for:

- <u>Kindle</u>
  $0.00
  or $8.00 to buy
- <u>Paperback</u>
  $12.00

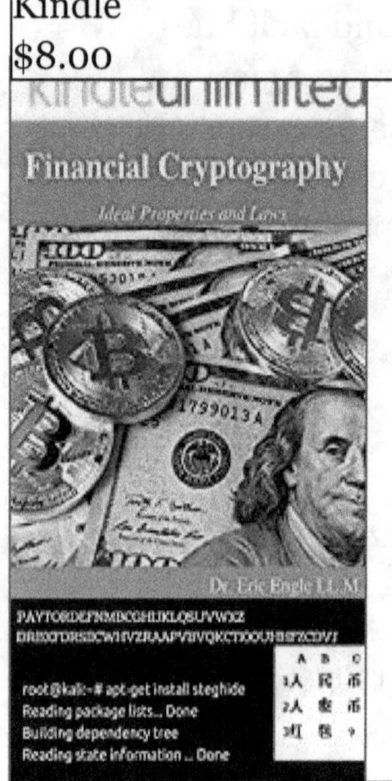

<table>
<tr><td>Kindle
$8.00</td></tr>
</table>

<u>Financial Cryptography: Ideal Properties & Laws (China, International Law, & Political Economy)</u> (Jan 19, 2018) by <u>Eric Engle (Author)</u> <u>http://amazon.com/author/quizmaster</u> Questions about the books to: eric.engle@yahoo.com Current financial cryptographic systems rely on asymmetric public key encryption. These cryptographic systems may not be as secure as is believed and suffer from certain weaknesses, some but not all of which are inevitable to any cryptographic system. Herein I propose an alternative cryptographic protocol for digital payments to enable legitimate economic functions of digital currency while evading risks of illegality to digital currency.

<table>
<tr><td>Kindle
$9.99</td></tr>
</table>

Can I Ask A Favor?

If you enjoyed this book, found it useful or otherwise then I'd really appreciate it if you would post a short review on Amazon. I do read all the reviews personally so I can write what You want! You can also write me an email with questions, comments, or suggestions: eric.engle@yahoo.com I really appreciate your feedback!

If you'd like to leave a review then please visit the link below: amazon.com/author/quizmaster

Thank you for your support!